2015 Hessler Street Fair Poetry Anthology

2015 Hessler Street Fair Poetry Anthology
each poem ©2015 by its individual author

Front cover photo
©2015 by Steven B. Smith
agentofchaos.com

Released 13 May 2015
as Crisis Chronicles #69
during The Hessler Street Fair Poetry Contest
hosted by Mac's Backs Books on Coventry
at the Ensemble Theatre in Cleveland Heights, Ohio
hesslerstreetfair.org
macsbacks.com

ISBN: 978-1-940996-20-2
1st edition, 2nd printing

The 2015 Hessler Street Fair
happens 16-17 May 2015
11 a.m. to dusk — rain or shine

All proceeds from the sale of this book help support
its publication and The Hessler Street Fair Poetry Contest
sponsored by The Hessler Neighborhood Association

Thanks to Shelley Chernin for her
last minute editorial assistance

Crisis Chronicles Press
John Burroughs, editor
3431 George Avenue
Cleveland, Ohio 44134
www.crisischronicles.com
ccpress.blogspot.com
facebook.com/crisischroniclespress

2015 Hessler Street Fair Poetry Anthology Contents

Alexis-Rueal — "Lard"
Michael J. Arcangelini — "Telling My Father about Paradise"
Dana Aritonovich — "I Realize It's Over"
Thandiwe Augustin-Glave — "My Heart"
Stephen M. Benefit — "You & Yours"
Cyndi Birkmeier — "Mom with Love"
Kim Boccia — "The Perfect Shade of Red"
Rose Mary Boehm — "*Heimweh* is more than a flesh wound"
Dianne Borsenik — "Flower Power"
Jeffrey Bowen — "for the godfather daniel thompson (1935-2004)"
Steve Brightman — "The Full of Eternity"
Christina M. Brooks — "Black River Falls"
Patricia Brodsky — "Almost Home"
Skylark Bruce — "Inside Pressure"
Chad Burrall — "Cold Memories"
Michael Ceraolo — "Mobservation #13"
Kathleen Cerveny — "Rosetta Stone"
Shelley Chernin — "How to Choose Sides in a Circular Argument"
Charles Cicirella — "Resurgence"
Caitlin Cogar — "Blowing Away"
Roger Craik — "Lake Erie Midges"
Subhankar Das — "She Hated Dogs"
Natalie Dickerson — "A Gift of Luck in the New Year"
Christine Donofrio — "Looking in the Mirror"
John Dorsey — "Steve Goldberg Death Poem"
Sean Thomas Dougherty — "Surgery"
Robin Wyatt Dunn — "Waiting"
Poetessa Leixyl Kaye Emmerson — "Diorama: The Persistence of Dreams"
Michael Fiala — "For Tamir"
Giselle Fleming — "The Night They Found You"
Diane Vogel Ferri — "Cleveland"
Ethan Fittro — "The Rose That Grew from Concrete"
Luba Gawur — "Kali"
Ken Gradomski — "Dream Driving"
Dana Grant — "Room"
Susan Grimm — "Questions for the Moon or the Moon Like a Shut White Eye"
Zachary Scott Hamilton — "Years in a Seahorse"
Austin Heath — "Yoshimitsu's Teeth"
Charles Hice — "Ici"

Veronica Hopkins — "1140 West 4th"
Christine Howey — "The Killer Turkey of Malabar Farm"
Preston & Paul Hrisko — "Ode to the Moustache"
Clarissa Jakobsons — "The Morning Wind Whispers"
Azriel Johnson — "Sentinels"
Krysia Jopek — "The City of Z"
Jeremy Jusek — "The Garrettsville Boardwalk"
Janne Karlsson — "Rock Bottom"
Diane Kendig — "Taking Daniel Thompson into Maximum Security"
Kim, theBwordpoet — "Left"
Ian Koenig — "Temptation"
Leonard Kress — "Jazz Chops"
Tom Kryss — "Cleveland Extension"
Craig Kurtz — "Informer's Catechism"
Lori Ann Kusterbeck — "Simple Ways"
Geoffrey A. Landis — "Shout"
Jim Lang — "Throat"
Jessica D. Lewis — "My Wrists as an Exit"
Lennart Lundh — "Elegy"
Caitlyn Lux — "The Cantaloupe"
Susan Mallernee — Haiku ["spring joggers"]
Marc Mannheimer — "The Same Chord"
J.W. Mark — "Expiring"
Molly McCann — "Summer Berry"
Bob McNeil — "A Versified Voyage"
Ray McNiece — "The Sun's Life Insurance"
Lila McRainey — "Silver Lining"
Philip Metres — "Compline"
Marisa Moks-Unger — "Lanterns over Lido"
Patrick O'Keeffe — "On the Back Page"
Mary O'Malley — "I Sit in Contemplation of Stones"
Ashley Pacholewski — "Ruby Slippers and Kansas"
Renee Pendleton — "The Strength of Weaving"
Tanya Pilumeli — "Ritual"
David S. Pointer – "The Lyrics Really Meant"
Sally Queen — "No One Can Hear Me"
Ben Rader — "Zombieku"
Valentina Ranaldi-Adams — "Irises"
Georgia Reash — "Love Beyond"
Poetess REDD — "Super Glue"
Elizabeth Rees — "Comfortably Numb"

rjs — "we won."
Amy Rosenbluth — "The Unraveling"
Elizabeth Rudibaugh — "The Soft Wind Blows By"
S. Renay Sanders — "Easter Shoes"
Heather Ann Schmidt —"The Star"
Erika Schoeps — "Shame"
Dennis Shanaberg — "Daylight Returns"
Kevin Frederick Smith — "Error"
Larry Smith — "Two Places at Once"
Steven B. Smith — "Daylight Savings Time"
Vladimir Swirynsky — "Brief History about Nothing in Particular"
Brian Taylor — "Silent Night, 1914"
Joseph Testa — "Why All Alone?"
Steve Thomas — "Heaven"
Jonathan Thorn — "Drifting Light"
Kerry Trautman — "Borrowing Your Shower"
Nick Traenkner — "Midnight. West Park Cleveland. April 16."
Mary A. Turzillo — "Sonnet 65,000,000 BC"
D.R. Wagner — "Gasping for Breath"
Mary Weems — "Blue Heron Sonnet"
Batya Weinbaum — After the Fight"
Laura Grace Weldon — "Earthbound"
Eva Xanthopoulos —"You Undid My Spiral Galaxy & I'm Still Dizzy"
Shkehlaht Yisrael — "Samot"
Janne Karlsson — "Grim Reaper"

Lard
by Alexis-Rueal

Don't look at that tub of lard like it's the devil.
Olive oil ain't got no place in a cast-iron skillet.
Not when there's cornbread to bake,
chicken to fry.
Yes, we still fry 'round here.
The country was made for sizzle and pop.
Grease for gravy.
Gravy flowing like water.
Like blood.
That same blood running through your veins, Miss City.
That blood that curdles at the whiff of a pig's knuckle
or the sight of a collard green.
City made you weak.
I know this.
I saw your cupboard—
That box of fake taters.
Don't even try to pass off fake taters when I come visit.
Or that tub of "I-Can't-Believe-You-Ain't-Using-Butter" butter.
Honey, I thought you were raised better than that.
I remember you and sitting at Granny's kitchen table
taking knife to spud, and I distinctly remember
you getting your fanny handed to you for dipping into
PawPaw's moonshine.
Don't try to tell me what your Doctor told you;
Mamma-Granny lived until she was 95 and she
knew how to use bacon grease and salt-pork,
and why did her rhubarb pie taste too damn good?
That's right. Lard.
Our family has ate good since a woman learned how
to blend meat with fire.
Since before the first tomato was drained
into the first Mason jar.
I still grow our grocery store in the back yard—
look our supper in the eye before I
put it on the stove.
I still know how to use a stick of butter and a tub of lard,
and I can still pronounce every ingredient of the meal I just cooked.
Now sit yourself down at the dining room table.
Supper's done.

Telling My Father about Paradise
by Michael J. Arcangelini

1.

"I can't even think of these as trees anymore," I told my father as we were driving past some Ohio woods — I'd just returned from my first trip to the West Coast and I was trying to explain to him about the immensity of the Redwood trees, the completely alien atmosphere beneath them and the otherworldly world that exists in the Redwood forests — I'd looked at the Ohio trees we were driving past and told him they didn't even look like trees to me anymore, they looked like bushes — "what's the matter with you boy," he said, "these are trees — they've always been trees — just because you been to California these don't stop being trees — they're just as good as anything they got in California," and I realized I had somehow offended my father while trying awkwardly to share wonder with him —

2.

We were riding down a freeway in Cleveland, Ohio, my father driving, both of us smoking — it was winter 1973 — when I finished my cigarette I reached over, opened the dashboard ashtray, which was perfectly clean, and stubbed out the butt in it — "what are you doing boy?" my father asked rhetorically — "just throw the damn thing out the window, don't mess up my ashtray — that's for turnpike toll booth change" — so I explained that where I had just been a few weeks earlier, in Southern California, the Cleveland National Forest, throwing a cigarette butt out the window could start a massive forest fire that could burn hundreds or thousands of acres — "I just can't throw them out the window anymore," I summarized emphatically — "well you ain't in California no more are you boy? and when you're in my car you throw 'em out the window" — the stunted trees of California's Cleveland National Forest exist in an environmental oven, a brittle tinderbox of beauty waiting to erupt and turn into smokey blackened acres of blight — my father, gesturing toward the wet winter landscape of Ohio, said, "you ain't gonna start no forest fire here" —

I Realize It's Over
by Dana Aritonovich

I realize it's over—
I'm in love again
with him again
different face
same man—
I only love one man
forever—
the same man,
in different shapes.

My Heart
by Thandiwe Augustin-Glave

My heart, it bangs to the beats of my step
The pump of my breath
The melody in my laugh

My heart it skips when I'm happy
Pulses when I'm mad
Leaks when I'm sad

They say it's the mind that holds the potions that are human emotions
But if that's true then why does my heart ache
When the earth quakes
The peace breaks

My heart feels
It feels

You & Yours
by Stephen M. Benefit

When you look in a mirror, it's what you don't see that's important.
The bounty on your soul is worth the content of your heart.
What you grasp today should have been cradled yesterday.
A favorite record spins the truth of your existence.
The consequence of you is a tin roof tinging in the heat.
The weight of a rose can bear on your imagination.
How do you hold the odor of what you said?
Your freedom lies in the scent of fallen leaves.
With every breath, you create the illusion of you.
The books you read reveal your beauty.

Mom with Love
by Cyndi Birkmeier

I will write you poems, mama,
now that you have gone.
The one you sent to me
with words of lavender,
dill, calendula, and lemon balm.
Tarragon and rose, I suppose,
words of luscious scent...
calming and content.

I miss you, mama,
while you are away,
and with my words, I pray
you know
that you are in my heart.
I will bring you lavender and rose,
mint and lemon balm,
and I should like to suppose
that you will hear this poem.

The Perfect Shade of Red
by Kim Boccia

Lipstick is essential,
In every woman's life.
Whether you're a lawyer,
Construction worker or wife.
Your desire is to look beautiful,
Hot and sexy too.
So you'll need the perfect lipstick,
Just anything won't do!
You slip into the perfect
Couture little black dress,
And with your four inch Pradas
You look good, you must confess.
There's just one thing missing,
That can turn everyone's head.
It's the, oh so important lipstick
That's the perfect shade of Red,
You have a lot choices,
But only one will do!
There's Bobby Brown, Sephora,
And Guerlain to name a few.
There's L'Absolu Rouge by Lancome,
But it has to be exact.
How about Lover by Chanel
That always has impact!!
There was this one time when
I wore Legendary by Smashbox
This guy walked straight up to me and said,
"Damn girl, you're a sexy fox!"
Although...that might not be the one for you.
Your features are quite unique.
Maybe you'd look better in
Ambrosia by Clinique!
There's so many colors out there,
Like Iconic, Retro, or Red Taboo.
It just has to be the right color,
That brings out the sexy in you.
I've also tried Rich Red, Hellbent,
And Fireworks by Dior,

Passion, Muse, Red Hot, Hollywood,
And I could name many more.
The point is, you have a choice to make.
No matter the outfit, leather or lace,
It's the lipstick the determines if,
You'll be sucking face!!
So make sure you wear "no smudge"
For smearing is what women dread.
And for God's sake woman, be sure to get...
"The Perfect Shade of Red"

Heimweh is more than a flesh wound
by Rose Mary Boehm

Geography is not important.
Everywhere
is the operative word.

Bared soul.
Barefoot.
Bare.

Tread carefully.
Mind your underbelly.
Be a turtle.

Carry the essence
in your holdall.
No roots allowed
past the security check.
They can see with
their X-ray machines.

You carry
a sharp, merciless
switchblade
made of stainless
grief.

Flower Power
by Dianne Borsenik

—for James

It's nasturtium
this evening, chili
with drizzling rain,
not the kind of weather
you're mint to enjoy
but to endure.
Here we go, taking
thyme to beet
the routine, to sloe down
and aloe ourselves
a night out; we can
dill with the dampness.
I mean, you have to draw
the lime between work
and play at some point.
We've bean busy,
and you can't curry on
without some kind
of break if you carrot all
about your sanity.
Lettuce fennel our
exhaustion into attitude,
pepper our lives with art
and entertainment;
lettuce go forth and
find some fun...
something will turnip,
I'm certain!
I lovage you.
These are the best daisies
of our lives...
you'd better bay leaf it.

for the godfather daniel thompson (1935-2004)
by Jeffrey Bowen

at the outpost coffee house you said, "you seem like a nice kid, now go away"
at the "together help line" it was, "hey kid, don't i know you?"
after a reading of some hot-off-the-press buddhist third class junkmail oracle jazz,
you advised, "try to stay out of jail," then offered your card, "just in case"

years later, down in kent, you got right in my face,
and said, "nice work, ever read at a junk yard?"

poet laureate, king of hearts, jack of the arts

tradesman, fisherman, great gray chief

bondsman, bread man, blanket man, thief

stealing time, and offering rhyme in return, you backed me into gigs:
"can you pick me up?" "got a minute?"
"what are you doin' right now?"
"any poems on you?"

so we did militant larynx, midnight poets, at the arabica, hart crane's valentine,
and readings in honor of d.a. levy and langston hughes,
PAND at cain park, dan's slam, luigi's in your ear, mark's reader,
barry's library, suzanne's book store,
on stage at CPT, hessler street fair, barking spider,
and gigs with sparks, salinger, melton, drumplay and brother ray

so when they say, "did you know him well?"
i say, "hell, every poet did"

and every one of the hundreds who actually went to church that day
had something to say, a poem to read, a story to tell

so, with a kiss of the ring and a wave of the hand,
i say thank you to the best damn poet in the land
of cleve,

from which, so many artists eventually split

but not you, daniel,
you stayed, and the band played,
and we all got paid
in smiles,
and miles of poems,
good deeds,
words to heed

and we still hear you in the wind
as it whips across the flats, cuts carefully up superior,
takes one-o-five to east boulevard, then jogs to juniper
whispers across the mic at the spider,
and playfully rustles leaves and tousles hair,
at the annual hessler street fair

The Full of Eternity
by Steve Brightman

Just like that, God whispered
to the feathered things;
let them in on the secret.
You think God doesn't know
just how good the apple tastes?
He told Myna, swore it to secrecy.
Swore on His son that if Myna
spilled the beans, then Myna
would spend the full of eternity
walking the earth like the dodo.
Myna didn't say a word.
Just laughed under his still-flighted wing
and watched the juices flow.

Black River Falls
by Christina M. Brooks

graffiti marked
below the city bridge
cast in hot sun and hard shadows
dandelions cast their golden crowns
knee high grass, litter strewn
the creaking trestle
wreathed in the bumps and groans
of turning wheels
the street side, hidden
a poet's graveyard of words
woven with ribbons on the fence
the colors reflected
in the nearby stream
where the black river falls

Almost Home
by Patricia Brodsky

For the Escaped Slaves Who Came North to Iowa

Beneath the even rows of stubble
in the autumn fields of my childhood,
under the unperturbed façade
of dirt road and feed store,
pasture and pond,
slept a proud history
no one told me about.
Early memories cling to the name,
like dry leaves
on a branch:
Libertyville.
A tiny cluster of houses
on the way from one place
to another.
Myself, restive,
in the back seat of a car
swaying along a humped gravel road
at the end of a long day;
outside the window an orange moon
juicy and creased
as a pumpkin.
When we passed through
Libertyville,
it meant that we were
almost home.
My great-grandmother's farm
south of town
is only a chain of fading images:
flour-sack aprons, smooth pine floors,
a wooden cradle with ribs like a whale,
my escape from the glare of a burning sun
into a coolness
safe and sweet as well-water.
Then on one visit, the last,
the murmur of aunts
milling in the shadows,

and in a back room,
someone dying.
The grownups said
the farm had been a station
on the Underground Railroad.
Where did they put the tracks,
I wondered?
I was a child.
I didn't know.
Autumn leaves,
a harvest moon
and a room full of shadows.
Fading images of chains.
Darkness like well water,
safe and sweet.
Figures milling,
on their way from
one place
to another.
Almost home.

Inside Pressure
by Skylark Bruce

There's a nod.
A knowing sneeze.
A shared headache.
We'd make a secret handshake
If we weren't already gripping
As many tissues as we knew we'd need.
Sinus you?
Yeah, sinus me, too.
The vast expanse of winter
Makes me forget.
The allergy-free masses
Start to cavort in the sunshine
And slog in mud instead of slush.
I cheer, too,
And then grab a wad of TP.
Your springtime ballads
Will be punctuated by my sneeze.
Sadly,
There is no relief
When winter returns for a late snowfall.
My sinuses are set on spring.
It's the worst of both seasons.
The pollen, spores, and dust
Are out of Pandora's tissue box,
Propelled with the force of her sneeze.
Sinus you?
Yeah, sinus me, too.

Cold Memories
by Chad Burrall

sunlight spun gold a hilltop away
rare and rich
amongst winter plated silver

blackbird elements on the snow
sung softly by
mill workers in their music

sycamores shiver Shawnee spirits
root bound canoes
sunk in streams of slush

stones knuckle down in cold hard ground
for they alone
recall the streaking speckled trout

Mobservation #13
by Michael Ceraolo

There was some doublespeak
on Earth called Right-to-Work,
                               and
it expanded skyward
                     Translation:
you had the right to work for less
anywhere in the solar system,
                               and
the right not to belong to a union
that could correct the situation

Rosetta Stone
by Kathleen Cerveny

On November 14, 2014, after a ten year journey, the European Space Agency's spacecraft Rosetta, successfully landed a probe on comet 67P.

        Beyond the blue November morning
where
        below
        cars scatter like beetles from
        under
        the lifted rock of night,
where
        the spikes of liberated trees
            pierce
        the impenetrable cobalt,
where
        the highway's Argus eyes have closed
                against the sun,
                      and later,
where
        the blue dome pales, troubled
        by the breath of jets, of yesterday's
        circumnavigated vapor—
            the resigned sigh
        of glacier's melt—

now
        the radio is telling tales of a machine
        of the imagination
            falling
        toward an assignation with a star
                shooting   deep
        in darkness colder
        than the coldest cold.
        that ever was,
where
        the keys to all the mysteries
            spin
            and pulse
                and orbit
        in our eccentric quest—
            the unrequited dream
                of who we are.

How to Choose Sides in a Circular Argument
by Shelley Chernin

You will not know where you are;
therefore, you will be lost.
Cling to the street sign
at the corner of Chagrin and Avalon
while you orbit the premises. Think
of King Arthur, whose sword was forged
where he would die. You will hear
hammers pang-panging out fabrications.
Ignore their false rings.

As you revolve, seasons will change.
Bring fur and assumptions. If you forget them,
you are near Sam's Fashion Post. No need
to feel cold or flustery. Be ready
for propositions. Guinevere accepted
Lancelot's and Mordred's. This,
either true or false. The subject is Guinevere,
but knights and villains are subjects, too.
Ponder the hidden predicate,

and if it is unsatisfiable, revalue
the variables. Take the No. 14 bus
to E. 14th and Prospect. It's a short walk
to Playhouse Square. Catch the matinee.
Near its conclusion,
Guinevere will sing, "I Loved You Once
in Silence." You will not be far
from where you were before; and therefore,
you will not know where you are.

Resurgence
by Charles Cicirella

why can't they hear it?

are they deaf? blind?
why are so many
resistant to change?
I love the seasons you
pass through like a
private investigator
rummaging through
old steamer trunks
looking for a phone
number that was
written on the back
of a matchstick

I remember Casablanca
Bob and I remember
Dooley Wilson singing,
singing for you like
you were Humphrey Bogart
I know you wanted to be him
stranded in some petrified forest
making time with the waitresses
like they actually understood you
and knew what it meant to be a legend
and not give a shit

you have always told us where
it was at and you still are telling us
why it is important to take a stand
because it's not dark yet, but it's
getting there and I'm afraid to let go
Bob I'm afraid you won't remember
how we sheltered each other from the
impossible storms in both our imaginative
and poetic visions, how we both agreed
Vincent knew what he was up against
and that if he hadn't taken his life we would

not be as acquainted with our own desires nor
would we give so much of a damn

the paint pulls us in as we turn our backs on
pressure cooker romance and all the self-medicated
responses she attempted before I convinced her
it's no good being a victim when your back is
up against the wall anyhow and any way you
slice it you are still going to have to enter the
eye of the storm before it is too late and all
the usual suspects are rounded up and later
dispensed with because every one of them
had a foolproof alibi, everyone but you Bob
your alibi was almost unbelievable in all its
deliberate and desperate fury

I wish we could shield each other from contempt
and I wish so much more was understood without
words or gestures of faith that faithless pedestrians
move through like ghosts with no fixed destination ...

Blowing Away
by Caitlin Cogar

In love with a silhouette, bathed in darkness,
which disappears from the doorway like an apparition,
never to return.
My heart leaves with you.

Even your shadow makes me crumble.

Crumbling...

I'm the crumb beneath your feet,
you're the agonizing thorn in my chest.
Someone explain how this is fair?
An injustice I can't digest.

You've joined an army of jokers,
chuckling at my expense...
But I tell you, I am much bigger than this.

Where did you learn to be so hard?
Jack Frost, you reign over me like a frozen tyrant.
With rock-solid features, you hide your emotions well
behind deliberate jet-black strands...
But I can read your insides.

You've cut me out of your life like a paper doll,
an innocent thing you can manipulate.
How fragile I am in your icy grip and you've taken advantage.
(What will it take to melt you?)
Look me in the eye, but don't say a word,
you couldn't do much more damage.

You aim to intimidate me,
and succeeded beyond your goal.
Mr. Big Shot, Mr. Too Cool,
never able to admit that
I instill the same fear in you.

You're a walking contradiction.

Always survival of the fittest,
too terrified to open up and show your soul.
You're not as fit as you portray.
I'll show you mine, if you show me yours.

It's such a shame...
you're too blind to see that,
more than anyone,
I "get" you.

Time is running out.

I thought I spotted a glimpse of
the ocean deep in your eyes...
A painful, pale shade of blue.
But now I know
that you're just as shallow
as a wading pool.

Hold your breath and count to ten,
maybe I'll go away.
Close your eyes and count to ten,
maybe we'll all just go away.
Turn your back and count to ten,
maybe it'll all just blow away.

Lake Erie Midges
by Roger Craik

All energy. No mouth.
Throughout the day – and day begins at five, or earlier –
this constant sliding at the air.

You're variously bugs, Canadian soldiers,
muckleheads.
John says you're really midges from the lake.

At any rate, one of you lands in my coffee.
As you stumble, trembly-slender,
back to life upon my hand

and as the last brown diamonds evaporate
to nothingness on you,
your antennae, fuzzed like wartime microphones, begin to move

and soon you're gone, restored
to anonymity,
traceless as air.

Often, at the eerie hour
when swallows jettison the sky to pipistrels
above the aerials and darkening roofs

I have seen you eddying
impervious in your gigantic swirls, a smudge dispersing then
regathering like smoke.

But one time, waking up before the birds,
before the mourning doves begin to crool
insistent-languidly their long unhurried syllables,

and shouldering on my dark green robe that fell
in folds around, its belt
swinging of itself into a knot,

I strode in slippers down my yard
to where the lawn gave way to woods

full-leaved but thickening still,

and looking up I heard a long unbreathing hum, a sound
of luminosity, of voices thronged
as one, and each one, as I thought,

insignificant.

But as I stood, and no leaf stirred,
it seemed that of itself the world began to turn
unearthly with your song.

She Hated Dogs
by Subhankar Das

She hated dogs.
So we locked us inside my study
as he barked outside
trying all the time to push the door open
with his head.

We were sitting on the lone single bed
facing each other and she said
I hate long hairs.
I smiled and opened the knot of my
shoulder length hair and let it flow.
Soon we started to suck the lips of each other
nibbling occasionally and allowing the tongue
to make its motions.
Then she got up on my lap
and caressed my long hair and said
I love your hair.
Will you love me forever?
I smiled and said yes
knowing all the time that
this forever will last hardly two hours
because once she is out of this room
she will never return.
She hated dogs.

A Gift of Luck in the New Year
by Natalie Dickerson

This little fat Buddha mocks with his laughter.
It's the New Year and his luck came late.
(Your luck ran out
before the sun came up 31 mornings ago.)
You gave him to me and we laughed—
We were fat on Christmastime.
But there's no peace on earth tonight.
There never will be.
In your studio the earth turns round and round
in your hands.
Do you whisper a prayer into those fat pots?
Once among the half-finished pieces
I found you everywhere.
I worked 1000 hours that week
and worked half of it for you.
Each time I counted the money I wept.
Each time I called, no answer.
Love, in the year ahead I wish you fat laughing luck:
If you are cold, I will wrap myself around you.
If you are hungry, I will spoon bacon grease into your mouth.
I will pour my blood into your veins to make you well.
Today, I rub his mocking belly.
Remember, from that day each minute brought more light,
the peaceful earth turns round,
and you cannot catch cancer like a cold.

Looking in the Mirror
by Christine Donofrio

I do not like what I see
I am own worse critic
My chin is double and my stomach hangs
Too fat for my own good but
I hold doors open for people and pray daily for those who have hurt me
I still like the concept of friends and believe there are good people out there
As you eat sweets the world will judge me
But someday as I look in the mirror I will not point the finger

Steve Goldberg Death Poem
by John Dorsey

one day i imagine they'll have
a parade for you

where nick traenkner will be
good and drunk
where old ukrainian men
will scatter paper roses
and sip the latest vegan soy ethiopian blend
harvested by young boys
for two weeks out of the year
in the summer sun

and how i will pour a thimble out for you
before going right back
to drinking instant
leaving my crushed styrofoam cup
on the corner of thurman
right next to a selection
of your finest berets
left out for the birds
to pick through
before flying away
for another season

Surgery
by Sean Thomas Dougherty

Forgot the red berries on the snow. Forgot how you were hungry but couldn't eat, and the nurse who never came soon enough with the morphine. Forgot the pain. Your pale face like a small moon. Your hair unwashed and unbraided, and all the papers they made us sign like citations. And the long walk from the parking lot in the snow, nervous I would not see you again, as I drove our daughters to school then rushing back across town to hold your IV'd arm. To wipe the drool from your mouth. And then more doctors, and the veins they couldn't find. The holes they left in your arms. And the tests that told us nothing. And then another surgery, and another, and another then it was time to go home, because we had one. With lists of appointments like citations, your limbs bandaged and bruised. Before we left, I glanced out that seventh story window, down at the street of strangers rushing off to the normal world we no longer belonged to—

Waiting
by Robin Wyatt Dunn

no what and when
the rain begins to send us down
under the sea
just you and me
abide our time
in these dangerous breezes
no revolution is as sweet as you

Diorama: The Persistence of Dreams
by Poetessa Leixyl Kaye Emmerson

Crescent moons hang by strings, unevenly spaced by
aluminum foil stars, glued to the navy night. Sparkling
glittery dust upon tops of trees made of cork and fine feathers.
The felt grass three shades green full of sour envy.
Double opal birds spread love songs inviting rhymes to
reason, branches to growth, roots to take ahold. Magnolias
whisper bitter broken faded nirvana in our bleeding ears.
Beauty marks the heart across the wild universe, pressing all
moments between finding North, yesterday, and this.

For Tamir
by Michael Fiala

Dear
Black
Child
of Cudell
your perfect youth pierced,
has seared the sacred heart
of Cleveland.

Proclaim a fast.
Call an assembly.
Tear our garments.
Mark with ashes

the crux of it: this black life matters,
stains blood permanent —
cries out from
cracked concrete, park play-ground.

Grief, loss, spark memory,
mother, kin,
re-membering
your face, bless-ed smile,
Missed.

and we,
we now are witnesses —
echo outcry, the vigilant sky, lament
shatters silence, disrupts the streets,
they arrest bodies, not the movement

truth-force, not brute force,
moment to moment,
make it plain

fierce love
stronger than death
calls your name,
calls you home,
to belov-ed community.

The Night They Found You
by Giselle Fleming

—*dedicated to Amanda, Gina and Michelle*

The Day they took you
You were walking home from school
You were coming home from work
You were taking a walk
And then vanished
We thought never to be heard from again

The Night they found you
We heard a voice from the past
We saw a new image to replace
The worn out missing posters
We met a new Good Samaritan
Whom we will always thank and never forget

The Day they took you
Turned into weeks, then months then years
Turned one woman's search into premature death
Turned numerous family members' lives upside down
Turned Missing Posters to faded images by the sun
The Night they found you
Your image was pale due to lack of sun
Your rights and body were violated but never your spirit
Your daughter was by your side

The Day they took you
Haunted by your countenance for a decade
Faded flyers replaced with fresh ones frequently
Candlelight Vigils and News Reports
Family and Friends still tirelessly searching

The Night they found you
A large teletype blared that you were found alive
Overcome with emotion
Crying myself to sleep
For what I instinctively knew you had endured

The Day they took you
Families prayed and never gave up
The Devil himself joined the search party
The psychic was dead wrong
As your indomitable spirit survived

The Night they found you
You rescued them all
Yourself, your child, your neighbor, and a stranger
You and the Samaritan did the right thing
And brought a happy ending to a horrific decade

The Day they took you
You never dreamed it would be a decade
You never thought to miss prom
You never thought to miss a wedding
You never thought many would think you were gone

The Night they found you
Reunited with Family
A new journey begins
You have showed us true bravery
And we will all now be able to heal with you

Cleveland
by Diane Vogel Ferri

I see Cleveland as a time not yet come,
a book we haven't read, the tenacious hope
of next year tangled in its bridges and highways,
beaming off the silvery water of a Great Lake.

A place where Christmas memories and food memories
are built into our bones, where you can step into a diamond
and hear an orchestra, or on any given day view a Rembrandt,
a Van Gogh, or hear poetry in a courtyard.

I believe in the Native Americans who named
our crooked river, the Traffic Guardians
welcoming you across the great divide of east and west,
into multicultural streets and towns.

In the jowls and crags of tumultuous industry
I no longer see smoke and filth - its former fame.
I see a place where Grandpa delivered ice, and
Dad played catch with a Cleveland Indian on the streets of the Heights.

God's good creation surrounds and envelops us
in the glorious greenery of the Emerald Necklace
that we wear so well, with the fearless changing
of the seasons flowing in our lifeblood.

The Rose That Grew from Concrete
by Ethan Fittro

—*inspired by Tupac Shakur*

Did you hear about the rose that grew from a crack in the concrete?
Finally saw the sun it feared it would never meet
The only hope the rose had was the light and its heat
But people are too busy to see the beauty beneath their own feet

Unnoticed the rose that grew from concrete goes
It doesn't care about the attention, it just grows
It does its best to make do, this isn't the life it chose
The concrete was tough and its damage shows

Those who do notice the rose that grew only see its damaged petals
They don't think about what it's been through, only where it settles
The other roses are beautiful, but they didn't have the concrete to wrestle
Still, the rose is just happy to feel the light, so in the sunshine it revels

See, the rose that grew from a crack in the concrete is you
The concrete is the struggle, which you need to push through
The sun is your motivation, the things you hope to one day do
But be proud of yourself, because damaged petals are beautiful too

No one notices the rose's hard work, just the results that come
Been through so much pain that at times it feels numb
People judge what the rose is, but forget what it came from
But a rose doesn't care what others think, it just wants to blossom

Kali: variations
by Luba Gawur

Red berries on white —
Drops of *kalyna* blood bend
boughs black over snow.

Red berries 'midst wintry fields —
Spots of blood upon snowy sheets ...
Kalyna boughing.

Crimson berries lay
on *kalyna* limbs...dripping
blood on white linen.

Kalyna berries
glistening on outstretched boughs
Kali nestled still...

Kalyna-Mother
beloved dark hoverer
Bittersweet virgin-bride...
Kali-roots spread wide.

Dream Driving
by Ken Gradomski

I drive the freight, the weight, the net, the tare... ahead, is it a
glacier wall or mountainside? In a dream I see skylight
from underneath my basement grate.
Light comes here with flurries of dust motes,
not unlike our deep sea trenches and their snowfalls of the dead...

It is an unedited video dream:
the scurry and flurry of a start-up business-office scene;
including painted secretary, deep-green schefflera plant
and an indifferent wife's cursory visit, badly timed
amidst chaos and the newly-delivered office furniture.

What is it then that still persists
to pierce my dreams
with magnetic longing?
Perhaps just the naked savagery I enjoyed...
Was I successful after all?

Marked up four hundred percent
I distributed only quality products
as a genuflection to some kind of juvenile, Arthurian honor.
Yet undershirts were always yellow
right underneath my arms;

wetted by tension, anxiety, rejection and my rabid unwillingness
to do the nine-to-five slavery
either in endless factory or corporate fiefdoms,
where all advancement hangs only on
the noble boss's whim.

...for a very long while all my heroes were barbarian warriors

Room
by Dana Grant

I didn't mean to lead you into an empty room, you see that room was once filled with dreams and magic pixie dust, I'm sorry I pushed you in and you had no choice but to walk across the broken shards of hope, I expected you to run away but I forgot your feet were bleeding too much, I left you there to see the broken parts of me, like the bloody panties of my rape at 15 and the knife I used to cut my wrist, I apologize for walking out and looking back at you as if you were already the past and I'm sorry that I locked your heart in this room, swallowed the key knowing that I would never return, I'm sorry I wasn't free for you, I apologize for presenting myself to you with bruised wrist and cut off feet, I wanted so much to see past the long talks and I'm holding on for dear life to truth and reality so I had to leave, I'm sorry I left an implied noose in that room, you see I expected it to burn along with those tragic memories, I do remember the good times, I remember the love, tripping over my untied shoes I race back there spit up the key, oh wait, I already forgot I have no feet, I open the door only to find an empty room once filled with dreams and magic pixie dust

Questions for the Moon or the Moon Like a Shut White Eye
by Susan Grimm

The wind rattles and presses
like a lover. It's all gravity and wings
now they've unpinned

the sky. Things flap. Birds call. Moons.

An angel might rip a hole in the rush,
step through.

With or without lily.
With or without buckler and sword.

Is there an announcement? Am I
dead?

Something about my womb?

It's never good news.

This urgent air. (What did one front
say to the other front?)

Skinning me slowly, coming in waves.

Years in a Seahorse
by Zachary Scott Hamilton

(1)

My mind is still a balloon full of helium. I am wandering the shale cliffs, I store a few balloons, and a dream, like a good idea, in your home. I found a glass of water in the forest vines, and filled my wandering legs without a doctor. When I arrive at your residence, seven seconds pass, using topics like healing with garlic, the state of the union, homelessness in the inner city, these make up an hour for me, and then abandoned, a few weeks. I figure if I sit down with you, and bring glyphs into your eyes, and the spinning summer waterfall bathing — I've forgotten about it — and the rest of Berlin unfolds with us, please notify the author Gertrude Stein right as six seconds (you seem pretty sure) are going through equations of creating that seven seconds stuffed in a box with a key.

(2)

Earthworms burrow three holes into 4465 East Remington Place. China plates, cabinet flower print, vine dreamt, a vertical ladder, tied at the top toe in painted sun, then the education of light. Healing a freeze-frame with two black fedoras, floating underwater, upside down in a profile, split in screens, two each side of a mule passing Arc Street digging glass with their new album, spectacles

o

like spiders, hospital and a queen's hand, glove-handkerchief umbrellas flying over the ocean; one, spinning nowhere, one in the rainbow. Middletown, turning a record beneath the needle claw, his wife closes herself in eyelashes.

Leprechauns climb out of old pottery all around the floating room. Middletown is a strange place, each bit of burning aroma wanders like tourists to the sea, the passage is in ocher locks of lichen, like arms. For a thousand breakfasts, in a claw foot tub, before moon and flame, bathing in leaves on the webs of sleep near the eaves of a French impersonator, Godfrey, with rockets in her dreams, large green eyes, and delicate hands, flirts with a tv remote. Her fingernails glitter in the static, dreams switch channels, static as she sleeps.

Closely trimmed in a white dance of basil lakes, and parasols that leak out speakers, the boats turn green. The algae, laughing, goat for halloween! Waking (A. in glove), (A. in goat) eating cakes. Godfrey samples small locks of her keyboard with knife-point algebra. The road lets in floating military backpacks, to wire with solder, and children and leaf the children's world, just left heart beat, just playback oxygen, oxen wanderlust.

(3)

Face the symmetrical furniture, the chandeliers, the jacket, the green, neon clock. The angel Auriel makes sure the favorite pair of color swatch eyes, the best way to the nose, woke eating cakes in the identical Wednesday, dancing on the slides is with a hundred years in this letter to the post office, or over a week , so galactic.

I am curious, humane, sheltered in scarves. I have grown a lot of wings from maple, and friends in New York. I even found a place for the past, and I will have a healthy fear of you who jangle your keys next to the passage in twilight. I join handmade letters from cardboard, kiss under heavens, float to shore, as Zachary.

(4)

At the felt sleeve of the cosmos, the Catalina stairways practice Eucla cod, the Elvers are fed atoms, and suspended in animations so the Danio can gorge on tv commercials.

There are nine awkward turns to go, thanks to the iceberg crystalline, her first frozen mammoths appear in the story bridge, and reflecting ponds, in the snow suits, and warm tongues.

(5)

Swerve into a hat, into a white whale, a bird, throwing glitter, glowing retina tin can, sewing machine spit, conditioner lathered foam noises. Lurching on a wire, a maple figure, is woven black threads, a new nightmare stitch under the winding of doors, sculpted all hair for songs, and gold furniture, rewind —

Yoshimitsu's Teeth
by Austin Heath

Undetectable by the naked eye,
you slip threatening euphemisms
[Bruce Lee yelps and noise]
into the softer parts of my body.

Sleepless unlike god-fearing mortals
drink wine fermented of kitchen tears,
fermented in Dixie cups
held closed by the pressure;
image of a social butterfly
with wings torn off by
childish tyrants.

Sneak into my tonsils
and tear out every crown
on your way to my lips.
Pillage and loot and riot,
bleed from the mouth.
Held together by wire.
Sewn shut with iron.

Eyes as two independent souls,
each a decoy of the other,
hidden, even to themselves.

Ici
by Charles Hice

see the sun comes
and it goes away
sometimes we get
rain
and
snow
sometimes life is pain
life can be like that
it is all okay
today
ici

1140 West 4th
by Veronica Hopkins

White walls, too much space, too many rules.
The alleged upper crust is brittle, inflexible, bland.
I don't belong here, or anywhere nearby (tried).
We move, down the street, across town, by the train tracks it's cheaper.
Material belongings mean less each year.
Badu said "pack light" and I know how right she is, spirit sister, blessed to be able to hear her.
I adore all the colors and find beauty where they told me not to.
Was never adept at processing the negative directives.
Bags for donations, suitcases for favorites that will one day belong to another or none.
This land is not mine; these streets teach me why the nomad is rich in wisdom.
I know how to keep moving, it's what I'll do until I join the dust and ash.
Home is in the heart, the wild and uncompromising heart, and in the embrace of my children,
wherever we are.

The Killer Turkey of Malabar Farm
by Christine Howey

I beg my father to tell the story
the one so bloody, grisly and gory
about the psychopathic bird of harm:
"The Killer Turkey of Malabar Farm."

At the moment I ask, dad's eyes glaze red,
I can tell the tale was true as he said:
the flightless monster that prowled the yard
and gave no quarter, a venal poularde.

Dad starts to speak, his fingers a-tremble
and shares the facts, no need to dissemble:
The tale of the girl, no more than fourteen,
turned into a relic from the Paleocene.

And the one of the husband, so bold and so brave,
who ventured out and had a close shave.
And then as he prided himself on escape—
a squawk, a slice, and they're hanging black crepe.

Among all the turkeys it was so hard to tell
which were benign and which one was from Hell.
They all looked the same, a most clever ploy,
hiding in plain sight, the turkey of Troy.

Too sad that youngsters are still so naïve,
tracing spread fingers because they believe that
drawing a turkey is just fun in the house—
and not the mug shot of a hit-and-run grouse.

So now when I tell my children the tale
of the feathered fiend that makes strong men quail,
I warn them never to be so blasé
about their dinner on Thanksgiving Day.

They should wish and hope the meat on their fork
was sliced from the beast , the devil uncorked,
the two-legged fowl whose bland looks disarm:
"The Killer Turkey of Malabar Farm."

Ode to the Moustache
by Preston and Paul Hrisko

O, Moustache how did you come to be?
Your history is a mystery.
You seem to grow so naturally.
And why do they call it pogonotrophy?

You are rooted in the past somewhere,
When men and women had facial hair.
The razor was not invented.
And women had no Nair.

Pubigerous cavemen wore you woolly.
Alexander none at all.
The walrus grows most fully –
Hail, the hirsute Neanderthal!

Moustache how varied in shape and size you are.
From a pencil-line to a bushy handlebar.
Chinese Emperors grew the Fu Manchus,
Centuries before the Howard Hughes.

Dali's was waxed and curled.
Twain wore his unfurled.
Chaplin disdained the fuller brush.
Gable's caused the gals to gush.
A blonde one died with Custer.
O, the life of the cookie duster.

When you smooch it kind of tickles,
But it's truly not your fault.
Because a kiss without a moustache
is like an egg without salt.

O, Moustache a question I moustache,
It's the ticklish dilemma of this ode.
Do I shave my two-week stash,
Or do I remain moustachioed?

The Morning Wind Whispers
by Clarissa Jakobsons

In a deserted mineshaft black throbs
against the white ceiling. Sunlight writes
on mountain flames, arctic breath seals
one kiss on her sleepless forehead.

The hallway vibrates dissonant steps
silenced by distant moons. She wakes
writes words before the kiss dissipates.
Premature swollen grief, satin tears
fade on each soft petal.

Sentinels
by Azriel Johnson

The guard shack is a poultry bird. Wings wide –
air moving through. We do not fly.

We are the sentinels
of the nightly – daily – weeklong – repetitious
fowl holocaust. My only consolation
is not observing the mechanical destruction
of genetically manipulated food.
Their only consolation is their ignorance
of what the outside world could hold.

The occasional escapee experiences
tiny freedom before being captured
by the ones "just doing their job."

My reverence is my apology,
"Thank you for your sacrifices."
Their comfort is someone paying
an attention which doesn't lead
to decapitation. I whistle to them
and they chirrup back to me. We all miss
the message. I don't speak chicken –
they don't speak hypocrite.

The City of Z
by Krysia Jopek

When you reach the stone gateway, do not be alarmed at the overwhelming grayness. It has been said generation after generation that the in inhabitants have sacrificed color to see more clearly the gradations of gray, the multitude of shades between fact and wish, past and future, truth and lies. Some say the villagers share a common genetic flaw and are, perhaps, color blind.

You will enter the city alone as few travelers are aware of the city's existence. Like the land of Atlantis, it is believed that floods and squall have carried the city away from itself, all record books and faded maps.

The old women who are missing teeth will smile their dilapidated smiles, for they will recognize you as invited, as chosen. Their kind eyes will meet your face and affirm that you are welcome without using any words.

Their fisherman husbands will turn their heads toward you but will not meet your gaze, less trusting than their wives, afraid of their dwindling catch. When they throw the octopus against the stone wall nearest the harbor to soften the meat for eating, only then will they steal glances at you, askance. It is better to pretend not to notice and continue on your way.

If a stray dog nuzzles your hand, it is okay to pet him. He, too, will know you belong and will accompany you through the labyrinth of broken porches and rusted swings.

After hours of walking, night will drop its velvet curtains, a sudden ending to the day's acts unfolding, Your eyelids will become the stone of the stone walls around you. Do not be alarmed that your sleep will be blank, that dreams do not exist within the city walls.

When you wake, the dog will lead you to the center of town where the clocks on the stone churches are set on different times, and bells chime randomly. Sit on the top step of the church with the clock perpetually stuck on nine hours and wait for me. I won't be long.

The Garrettsville Boardwalk
by Jeremy Jusek

The wood grain is like fingerprints,
coarse DNA of this rattlesnake town.
I know when to lift my hand
to avoid splinters.

The brick wall behind Subway,
ivy-hugged, propped our shoulders
when I— during my— that kiss.

I remember the sloppy
half-moons of her lips
like punctured tangerines.

Eagle Creek splashes bubbling
code. The finest cryptographers
could learn a thing or two
from our pickle farmers.

Under the walk, biology students
carve holes in the ecosystem
with nets and formaldehyde jars.

Minnows dart around their bare
toes. Mine have five hundred feet
to walk with nowhere to go.

the cliff leading
  down
to rock bottom
  is paved with

shame
  guilt
    white knuckles
  and

    desperation.

Taking Daniel Thompson into Maximum Security
by Diane Kendig

Daniel had wanted to go with me, and I had held off, held back, held on to the slim ribbon of credibility I had ridden in on for sixteen years. Many other writers had ridden in with me—Gloria Naylor, chain-smoking like a bad carburetor those days when smoking was permitted; Joe Bruchac and Randy Bates, who'd seen it all, gliding in, cool as Akitas; and Okantah, wearing dreadlocks a decade before they were hip and carrying a huge African drum which I had no paperwork for, eventually walked right in with his instrument.

"Daniel," I had said to myself, "he'd be the last writer I'd take into prison." Bring the court jester of poets? Storied for his stint in the Cleveland jail for some protest, demanding herbal tea and vegetarian food, loved by the judge who happily slapped him with a sentence to give poetry readings Daniel gladly served, till the police gave up charging him. Prison, I kept telling him, is a place where jokes don't fly.

Then at the end, serving what inmates call my "short time," I decided he *was* the last writer I wanted to take into prison, but I flitted like a scared bird. "Listen, Daniel," I said on the phone. "This is maximum. It's not funny. If you fuck up, they won't touch us but my writers won't meet again." I know he circled his eyes to the ceiling and thought, Talk to the hand, Diane.

But when he arrived, I saw he had aged, fretted over dental hygiene he was committed to after years of neglect. And entering the prison that night, he could have been a chaplain, so piously quiet, all joking left roadside. I can't tell you how badly Daniel wanted into *that* prison. We made the half-mile walk to the concrete meeting room, set up, and he read—though if you know him, you know he *said*, not read: he chanted and cooed, then raised and raised his voice and ranted. I have to tell you, that I have never heard Daniel so loud and clear, despite his age and weariness, about six months before the first cancer diagnosis, despite reverberations off floors and walls. He gathered up everything he had been writing for and against all his life, injustice and hurt, all the broken letters of the earth, love's new light he still held out for, and man, he said them off while the inmate artist penciled a sketch of him, clear as a black and white glossy. Daniel began with *Those in power always want / those in poverty to live on poetry*....

The guards gathered in the back, first a gray shirt, then several, then several white shirts. It was about 7 o'clock—how could there be that many white shirts left that late? I thought well, this is it: we are about to be ousted—until I noticed that the guards were applauding loudest of all, that in fact, they loved Daniel's hymn to the veterans in the marketplace, *black-toothed, crew-tattooed, blue, open flies, eyes of salt and humor surviving / Wars and rumors*, his complaint about justice as a railroad. Most of them are vets, see how justice is a railroad. The guards did take exception to his Dillinger poem and one shouted, "But he *did* shoot the deputy." In Lima, they know their Dillinger.

I know what people say about prison, that everyone has a lot of time, that they have nothing better to do, which is not true, and in fact, there is much more worse to have done to you and to do, and no one was wasting a minute in that room as Daniel took us all into the purpose of poetry, which, as another dead Ohio poet said, is to break our hearts. Men wept.

I should add that I took Daniel out of prison too, and that was harder, except he was tired and even he did not want to *sleep* in prison. I didn't know that it would be the last time I'd see him, but I'm glad this is my final memory of him: finally free, out and on the road. I drove, he rode shotgun, his right arm along the open window, chuckling as he repeated, "But he *did* shoot the deputy" the long ride home that exceptionally warm and starry autumn Friday night when Daniel took the prison.

Left
by Kim, theBwordpoet

She could have been a model.
Her sweet brown skin shining in the lens
Her face relaxed in seduction
Her body contorted in the name of artistic lust.

She could have been an artist.
Her pretty painted fingers running over the blank canvas
Her vision becoming the world's reality
The instruments slaves to her mind's eye.

She could have been a teacher.
Her story teaching others to love
Her interpretation bringing youth clarity
Her presence causing first time wets and hards.

She could have been my equal.
Her lips succumbing to mine
Her body waiting for my forbidden fruit
Her heart free, and full, and open.

What she is is a grocery clerk.
Trapped in a dead-end pick and swipe
Barely making enough to live terribly
And therefore submitting to society on the side.

What else she endures is being stuck with a guy
Who keeps her in terrible tearful ignorance
Who's going to leave her high and dry soon
Which will most likely cause her forever scarring...
When she could have been mine.

Temptation
by Ian Koenig

I see you from across the room
My heart stops
Never in my life had I seen anything quite like you
Your elegance, your curves
How could I be so naive as to let you slip by
No
I can't
I won't
Everyone would see
How ashamed I would feel knowing I had one at home
Waiting
But how torn I would feel knowing I let you slip through my fingers
Tempting
Your perfect form is so divine
I can't help it
You devil
I stand up and walk over
I imagine the way you would taste on my lips
Four feet, three feet, two feet, one
"Excuse me,
I'll have the glazed donut with sprinkles please"

Jazz Chops
by Leonard Kress

Too many years ago
    I'm dragged by my friend Joe
now a kippah-wearing orthodox Jew
    living with his 5 kids in a new
illegal West Bank settlement
    into what is the cleared bargain basement
of the old Snellenberger store
    in Philly, turned community college—to hear
young Byard Lancaster
    blow his alto sax faster
and better than any I'll ever get to hear
    again. Earlier this same year
I coax my reluctant high school girlfriend
    to lie to her parents who don't trust
me or her, up to the Village Gate
    before it is too late
to hear Pharoah Sanders. We have to spend
    the night as fire rages next door and pumpers pinned
my car to the curb. The conflagration nothing compared
    to his sax solo or her father's rage, teeth bared
when we finally return, still shaken and brought
    to tears by his group's hour-long *Jewels of Thought*.
Decades later I drive my daughter, not quite three
    to the indoor city playground we
visit weekly, our mutual treat
    where I can take a perimeter seat
and read and she can trike
    and pretend-crash & gas-up and circle back
between snacks. To reach it we head toward
    Columbia Ave, hang a left on 33rd
and pass the cracked row house
    where Coltrane lived for a spell, to pause
and read the plaque and decipher the peeling
    mural, avoiding the dealing and double-dealing
in the neighborhood, named—as if it's a classic tune
    we sing to our kids in 5/4 time—*Strawberry Mansion*.

Cleveland Extension
by Tom Kryss

The bridge is elevated at signal, in advance
of the crossing, then lowered and locked down
as he yanks an arm through windbreaker,
locks up the control tower, and half-runs
down the metal stairway to his car and drives
to the next bridge. As the freighter approaches
he flicks the series of toggles that set down
the barricades, and again lifts the moveable
road into the night, waits, and brings it back down,
in sections. A telephone rings and keeps ringing
with no chance of being answered : the tender
of mechanical bridges is already speeding away,
swerving up and down alleys to the third
and final bridge. He takes it up slowly, lights
a cigarette, leans, peering over the beam
of light at the sides of the vessel : Duluth,
and a scrap of graffiti picked up in one
of the harbors, in a year that no longer exists.
Then, after securing the tower, he returns
over broad platforms of steel let down
like a series of coats over water in approximations
of courtesy towards a lady's advance, returns
to the primary station — twelve-inch television
had remained lit in his absence : The Late
Show, regarded for a moment in astoundment,
then punched off. Alone now, as ever. Not
a single instance of automotive traffic during
the multiple operations, and reflections in the waters
below, long exposures of starlight, weave on
undisturbed. River traffic itself declines
every year and there has been talk of automating
the bridges, which even now marshal the unified
incomprehension of thundering lizards reared
in confusion and awe at a comet's approach.

Informer's Catechism
by Craig Kurtz

Left or right,
it's all the same;
when they squeeze you,
you'll give a name.
It's done for a hit,
it's done for a meal;
so someone gets nailed,
so what's the big deal?
Ethics are swell,
but only up to a point;
it's you or them, matey,
facing time in the joint.
Sure you feel bad,
but what can you do?;
informers are people —
they have feelings too.

Chopping up the logic's
just a matter of degree;
when they come a-knocking, pal,
it's either you or me.
It's done with lousy dollars,
it's accomplished with dire threats;
when they haul you off
I'll be the first to send regrets.
You'll do it for a smoke,
you'll do it for a drink;
it's nothing personal, you know,
so who you calling fink?
Talk all you want 'bout principles
or saving your own skin;
informers have fam'lies to feed —
that's why you got turned in.

You can do it for religion,
you can do it for the flag;
just make sure your reasons
will fit the size of a toe tag.

You can do it for the war,
you can do it for world peace;
whatever works for you
will also work for the police.
What you call necessity
I call base cowardice;
but what we all fall back on, is:
mind your own business.
Ten years is what I got
for your rotten bowl of soup —
best wishes from your chums
at the informer's support group.

Simple Ways
by Lori Ann Kusterbeck

he said it in the simplest way possible
just a few words
sprinkled
a dusting of confectioners' sugar upon the page

he picked
every syllable
with precision
assembling them together
like notes on a staff

a place
a syncopated rhythm for each one
he beautifully broke every beat and meter
like a host breaking bread at his table
  not a crumb wasted
  not a word misplaced
  not a pause or a breath untimely
  not a crust of content misused or erased

he found his literary path
uncluttered with clichés
instead
he chose
the less beaten path
his poems gently kneaded
artfully composed
folded over and then exposed
a much simpler way

Shout

by Geoffrey A. Landis

I have to shout.

I have to shout
inside my head.

I have to shout
inside my head
to drown out the voices.

I have to shout
inside my head
to drown out the voices
of sanity and reason.

I have to shout
inside my head
to drown out the voices
of sanity and reason
so I can reach the madness.

I have to shout
inside my head
to drown out the voices
of sanity and reason
to reach the madness
in which genius is hidden.

Throat
by Jim Lang

instrument of sing
& swallow—toss off a throw
out in inside out—

My Wrists as an Exit
by Jessica D. Lewis

I used to have dreams
That my wrists were an exit
I don't any more

I used to think, thinking often:
I'll open that door, but not today.

When days were bad, and conditions not ideal
It brought me a great deal of comfort to think about leaving
    through that exit. And not having to return to shut the door.

Elegy
by Lennart Lundh

Dig the small grave
and place the smaller body so,
just so. The chill May rain
and the warm human tears
falling on her head
will serve for the ritual
washing of this pup,
barely two days old.

Some future digger after truth,
alien or human, kneeling with
trowel and brush at this grave,
will note in clear, careful script
the wonder that a people would
be so deliberate with the smallest
of their gods' creatures,
and so careless of themselves.

The Cantaloupe
by Caitlyn Lux

Grown from the blossoming bud of a gnarled vine,
Grown from a contorted bed of greenery,
You blossom into an elliptical sphere,
Resting on the cool ground,
Like the cratered moon that hangs in the cold abyss.

You are a golden globe that is rough to the touch.
You are coarse sandpaper with an unforeseen twist.
You form a shielding layer to hide your sweet surprise.
You possess smooth, glossy flesh that glistens in the sun.

Your bitter rind disguises the goodness that lies beneath;
The peach-tinted center, the vanguard of all its parts.
You awaken my taste buds and excite my nose.
Your nectarous flavor makes you a candy of nature.

When squeezed,
A liquid of gold,
A flow of syrup,
And an aroma of citrus
Spill onto the plate below.
As a capsule of sunlight,
As a vessel of delectable treasures,
You become a confection of the earth.

Haiku
by Susan Mallernee

spring joggers
in shorts
wintered white

The Same Chord
by Marc Mannheimer

I saw the purple first
crocuses cost winter its end
and spring, newly consummated
...the fog on my glasses
the frost on the car windows
breeze biting into my morning skin
green buds daring to show their kindness
all of the trees seeming to ache
the same 3-tone chord, sustained
— seek, grow, pass it on

Expiring
by J.W. Mark

dominion calls
her kingdom come
endeavor's loss
she greets

appearances for mourning, light
fluorescent dims to chill

like bacon,
eggs
and breakfast
meats

indifferent
tossed
for waste

Summer Berry
by Molly McCann

Radiant ruby domes overlap
Each holds a single drop of juice,
Combining to give the taste of sweet bliss.
Tiny hairs poke from in between
Like rays of sunlight penetrating the clouds.
Fresh and fragile
Yet bursting with flavor.
Summer berry where are you?

The center is a cavern
Like a black hole
Holding the spheres of taste inside.
Reverse infrastructure keeps the raspberry from collapsing,
The outer wall soft and squishy,
It shines as if light inside is trying to escape.
The inside speckled with tiny seeds.
Summer berry where are you?

The red raspberry is a beach ball
Easily floating through the shimmering sky.
Succulent and dripping with crimson juice
The aroma travels like a light breeze on a summer day
Bubbles congeal to form this heavenly fruit
Like the foam resulting from the crash of wild waves
The berry is a beacon of leisure and optimism.
Summer berry where are you?

A Versified Voyage
by Bob McNeil

Another boy was raised at the Hudson River
  With a firm Earth Sign—
  A promising limb on an African tree—
  And The Thinker, his archetype,
  Sat beneath his unburdened brow.
24 seasons later,
  The child scrutinized
  The Lost Tribe's Jerusalem—Harlem.
  And like East 127th Street's Shakespeare,
  Langston Hughes,
  The boy embraced his race.
At 54 seasons,
  The boy became a knowledge-consuming entity
  Learning about African-rhythmic prose, odes,
  Bantu, Zulu, Malinke, Yoruba,
  South of the Sahara songs.
The child traveled
  The geography of his mentality
  With David Diop, Dadie,
  Césaire and Senghor,
  Poets who created the seeds
  That became Afrocentric Breeds.
To the boy,
  These poets were sight-igniting keys.
  By plying those keys,
  He opened doors to vistas
  Where Black people were birthing
  A renown-bound future.
Eluding adult's brimstone-sizzling stress,
  Beneath a dirt-antiquated tree,
  He studied comfortably
  And saw the spirits of the pundits.
At 55 seasons,
  With his ever-present pen and paper,
  He was runner-in-a-race-inspired—
  Those were his sight-igniting keys.
  By plying those keys,
  The child and a page converged
  And an aged griot emerged.

The Sun's Life Insurance
by Ray McNiece

The Pacific carries
no health insurance.
Brazil's rain forest makes
even less than minimum wage,
silver dripping last rusty branches,
and Greenland's glaciers rely
on no trust fund interest —
business as usual, ashes, ashes
dusting the picture window.

The ozone layer retains
no high powered legal team
and cannot read the fine print
of cancer etched on skin,
The Great Barrier Reef
has no warranty on its shelf life,
and what profit if plain old dust wins
another academy award —
business as usual, ashes, ashes
coating the high definition screen.

That ragweed between concrete
wilting, will not receive
this year's Nobel Prize for Science,
migrant warbles will not return
to condos called Whispering Woods —
no woods, no whisper —
and the Sun's Life Insurance does not cover
pre-existing conditions including
black holes, quasars and cosmic breathing —
business as usual ashes, ashes
lightly falling lightly as snow.

Silver Lining
by Lila McRainey

At first newborn blush, we all shine.
We furiously rub each other so frequently,
we fairly gleam with the highlights of love.
But like fine silver, polished endlessly over time,
worn spots appear, or not enough care and we tarnish.
The chemical smell of rotten eggs leads the way back to
blessed perfection.
Yet if we take meticulous care of love, the
neglectful rot we will never have to suffer again.
The inevitable thinning of our silver lining is
simply proof of our preciousness in the determined,
hopeful, greedy hands and eyes of an irreplaceable
lover.

Compline
by Philip Metres

That we await a blessed hope, & that we will be struck
With great fear, like a baby taken into the night, that every boot,

Every improvised explosive, Talon & Hornet, Molotov
& rubber-coated bullet, every unexploded cluster bomblet,

Every Kevlar & suicide vest & unpiloted drone raining fire
On wedding parties will be burned as fuel in the dark season.

That we will learn the awful hunger of God, the nerve-fraying
Cry of God, the curdy vomit of God, the soiled swaddle of God,

The constant wakefulness of God, alongside the sweet scalp
Of God, the contented murmur of God, the limb-twitched dream-

Reaching of God. We're dizzy in every departure, limb-lost.
We cannot sleep in the wake of God, & God will not sleep

The infant dream for long. We lift the blinds, look out into ink
For light. My God, my God, open the spine binding our sight.

Lanterns over Lido
by Marisa Moks-Unger

They were there hovering,
incandescent above the ebb tide.
Stirring, living sparks
twice lit by flame and moonlight.
One by one, lifted on the gulf breeze,
Vesta herself may have swept them into the air —
Lilting along, souls of fire in paper frames,
Lanterns lifting from eight to ten to two
Passed celestial dials into the night.
Marked by the rising of Jupiter,
the Little Dipper. The setting of Mars.
Into the heavens. Into night's moth-eaten veil.

On the Back Page
by Patrick O'Keeffe

Yesterday's *Sandusky Register*
spread out under fresh cat litter
turns up news on the back page.
Dwight Rawlins. Survived by wife Lucile.
Two children. Three grandchildren.
All in Sandusky. A half-sister in Tulsa.
Dwight Rawlins. Last seen
through a man-door square of glass
as we made sure he left the premises.
Sat a while in his car—door ajar—
on the edge of a worn vinyl seat
legs hung out as if steel-toe shoes
were somehow stuck to the asphalt space
he'd parked on for thirty-seven years.

"We should call the cops—
what if he's got a real gun?"
While crooning a Johnny Cash hit suddenly
he'd pulled a twenty-two caliber pistol
from his pants—a starter's gun—
emptied all its blanks into the air.
Humanity scattered. Scurried for cover behind
machinery and a stack of wooden pallets.
"It was only a joke," he'd exclaimed
arms out—workman hands pleading.
Tears flooded the crags of old cheeks
and turned tired blue eyes
enlarged through safety lenses
into running sores.

That day we never did call the cops.
Dwight never did come back in and kill us all.
He finally just folded his legs up
closed the car door and drove home.
Dwight Rawlins.
Who no longer sees
through magnified blue eyes.
Whose workman hands no longer work.
Toothy mouth no longer sings
a favorite Johnny Cash song.
In his place empty space rings
with silence.

I Sit in Contemplation of Stones
by Mary O'Malley

Somber stones sit down on earth

stars will shine with bolts of joy.
An old birth is pulled to life
truth and mercy become joy.

I sit on the silent stone large
and huge. I feel the sun on my haunches green and orange.
The quiet wake of heaven's barge
floats on Lake Erie. Dirges are song, which become
songs of last loss.

Tonight I will change gray to gold, dark to light.
Understanding brought forth into my simpleton's mind
while cascading nanos of information
become blossoms inside my head.

Winter will be cleansed, fires smothered and put out
peace reign down from the time seeded clouds.
Water flow at a balanced pace.
Sky will suffer no harm.
Sun will appear on schedule,
air pristine and cleansed.

Ruby Slippers and Kansas
by Ashley Pacholewski

Somewhere over the rainbow

Dorothy is clicking her heels together,
thinking that "there's no place like home"
while victims of broken promises search for the yellow brick road.
Concealing insecurity with smiles,
throwing empty laughs into the air,
like Professor Marvel, they magically cloak their sadness and show no one
    their despair.

How do you tell Dorothy that Glenda isn't real?
Don't expect the Good Witch of the North to present you with those heels.
They're not "one-size fits all"
And they certainly don't shine;
Auntie Em and Uncle Henry: they're a delusion of your deceitful mind.
Where are your mom and pop?
Even 1930's Hollywood understands that a "real family" is a filming flop.

Dorothy has serious problems.
But so do millions of victims searching for that yellow brick road.
They are busy falling from one of Kansas's many Twisters.
Ripping through families like the Cowardly Lion escaping his worst fears.
Fear insatiably searches for more troubles to fill its cravings while
Rust continues to look for the Tin Man's heart.
Troubles don't melt like lemon drops,
they freeze like the Scarecrow trying to do a simple math problem.

Somewhere over the rainbow,
Dorothy realizes that no matter how far she's traveled,
Everywhere is damn Kansas.
And Dorothy's heart, (she knows she has one because she can feel it
    breaking) tries to break out of her ribcage and scream.
Miss Gulch is always present detecting problems,
complicating fears, and creating more cyclones.
Dreaming never makes bluebirds fly.
And just when Dorothy thinks that all hope is lost,
it doesn't float down from the sky in a bubble blown from God,
it simply arrives on her worn down, last ounce of sanity.

Everything she's looking for
has been right here all along.
She is more capable of more than she knows
she's always had the power but had to learn it herself.
Listening to the last whisper of the wizard's advice,
she launches the shoes off her feet into the Twister
and wakes up surrounded by the debris of Red Poppies.

Out of Oz and into Kansas,
she builds her own yellow brick road.
She carefully lays each brick,
determined to make her own path.
Cradling each block like the last of her most precious dreams
she covets her work.
This path will not end with a wizard,
but with whatever wishes she once wasted on those ruby slippers.
Dorothy learns that courage doesn't always roar,
that sometimes courage is the quiet voice at the end of the day saying,
"I will try again tomorrow."
Because if happy little bluebirds can fly beyond the rainbow,
Why oh why can't she?

The Strength of Weaving
by Renee Pendleton

taut as warp
you steel against my weft
that wreathes around
your stiffness
in and out
the knot that binds
will loosen on its own
you say
you pull away
hold firm
wait for the slackening
as if you didn't know
the strength of weaving
is in the tension

Ritual
by Tanya Pilumeli

As a child I would press the heels of my hands
into my eyes at night to watch the lights.
I waited for visions, like flesh-colored
TV guides left on the coffee table, each page
crinkled from spilled water.
Out of the quiet stillness of my skull
I could count on wild epics of dark matter,
the whites of eyes staring back from under my lids.

But no one ever saw my circus, its shaded reds,
handprints and spilled doubloons. It wasn't listed,
so their sets showed snow and collected dust.
Eyes were used for deciding which paint to pick
or to find knives to set the table or not at all.

And it didn't matter even then that I had a canopy bed
with light pink flowers and yellowed lace.
Or that I hung my scapular and rosary on the bedposts.
My Bible was always flipped to Revelation.

The Lyrics Really Meant
by David S. Pointer

Bullfighter lighter fluid deconstructed
by digital brush strokes, approved by

overseas fish and game alliance, close
to auctioning off Otto Dix memorabilia

combating artistic brutality, engulfing
creative flock obscurity squeezing into

over marginalization boiling underneath
an atomic montage, vaguely symbolic,

supercharged, calculated for sonically
discussing diversionary newscast bits

melting mid-song to much whiter flame

No One Can Hear Me
by Sally Queen

Sneaky sneaky Autism always lurking about,
Causing my body to move awkwardly with some random shouts.
I wonder what you're pointing at, but I'll keep trying til I get it,
Who touched the bathroom light switch? I'm not playing, who did it?
I need to hear this Elmo sing this song just one more time,
And I know it's scary, but trust me I am fine.
I flap to burn my energy because I am just so excited!
And I understand you're funny, I just can't tell you that I like it.
I know I ate all mine, but I was hoping you would share,
And when I can't control my body I'm hoping you won't stare.
I try to work so very hard because I want to bring you joy,
Sometimes I think they forget, I am still a little boy.
I love, I hug, I cry and I play if you just give me the time of day.
I struggle, even with snuggles, please just don't give up along the way.
Sneaky sneaky Autism always lurking about,
I'm still headed where you're headed, I just choose a more colorful route.

Zombieku
by Ben Rader

I roll your eyeballs
on my palm then crunch your arm
this is one sweet date

Irises
by Valentina Ranaldi-Adams

Noble ladies dance in frilly, pastel petticoats.
A subtle breeze disperses their luscious scent.
The gentle rain adorns them with crystal beads.
Unseen soldiers protect them with elongated, green swords.

Love Beyond
by Georgia Reash

She waits for me, my mistress pen;
My secret lover;
My bold abandon to
Language lines and swirling tempo.

She waits until she can wait no more
And then she will rush to me having
Finally had the chance to breathe again
Into the synchronicity of words.

And we cling and claw as I work to master
Insufficient words into sufficient meaning;
The dance of hidden passion eking from my soul and into my hands
Hoping that maybe a poetry, a story, a narrative will tickle.

I call on her, like an ancient Goddess that empowers; NO,
like a Goddess that releases me into my true and
Natural flow. And when print and mystery collide in me,
I have created an invitation to
Join with.

Here, I mate with everyone and with Universe
And I must in order to live.
When can I dive into her? Let her? Take me?
When can it be she and me alone again?

Shackles still attach to me; chains of jobs that squeak
Like rusty bike chains and mean even less.
Let me live more freely in that original flow
Of penmanship.

With her in the shadows of my darkest
Tunneled lines of truth telling,
Always there,
I exist in real form.

Super Glue
by Poetess REDD

I see you

Standing there, tall and strong

A soldier ready for any battle

Tears?

I am surprised you allow your essence to flow so freely

But covered in its warmth I feel safe

Your tears easily bond the pieces of my broken heart once strewn about like a child's discarded jigsaw puzzle, just an undistinguishable blur of colors and shapes, now a beautiful picture appears full of depth and breadth

I ask,

How do you maintain your strength?

You answer,

Hold me tighter.

Your masculine scent fills my nostrils, so strong I can taste you

Never have I felt so safe

Never again will I feel alone

And I thank you

Comfortably Numb
by Elizabeth Rees

Not high, not low.
No joy, no sorrow.
Consciously aware but immune to the pain.
There is safety in the solitude and quiet.

I exist in the periphery.
I tiptoe on the outskirts.
Visible from a distance,
Details unable to be seen.

My burdens remain unshared.
My struggles my own crosses to bear.
I am my own most reliable friend.
My comfort and strength comes from within.

Wounds can heal without words.
Life can be lived alone.
Contentment can be found in the ordinary.
Magic was never promised to anyone.

we won.
by rjs

listen to the president:
we won.

there's no water in the desert.
we won.

the wetlands in the gulf are slick with oil.
we won.

the noon sky is black,
blotting out the sun;
we won.

the fires will burn for months.
we won.

the generals are giggling:
we won.

a hundred thousand bodies
are rotting in the desert;
we won.

god bless america.
we won.

The Unraveling
by Amy Rosenbluth

It must start somewhere— either from the top or the bottom.
Pull at it just a bit more and the ball wound tight starts to spin—
it isn't a bad thing, just another object out of control.

Unraveling— the opposite of a tumor wound tight in the brain—
It is a coming undone, maybe has been for some time now, but still.

I try all sorts of tricks to stick the ends back together—
Using spit like glue, taping it up with well-made plans and a future
 without any frayed ends.
But still, it is unraveling and I am there watching in a sad state of horror.
It is the looseness of the spiral that is so disorienting.
Not knowing which direction it will turn, in which direction I will be turned.

There is only room for faith the length of twine, as it unwinds.

The Soft Wind Blows By
by Elizabeth Rudibaugh

Rocking in the garden
The soft wind blows by
Cascading green ribbons through the air
Floating along the breeze
Tickling tiny babies
The sweet smell of summer
The soft wind blows by
Rustling the sticky grass
Rushing past the stars
Opening our eyes to imagination
While closing them to reality

Easter Shoes
by S. Renay Sanders

On Palm Sunday Eve
She was breaking in
Her Easter shoes
Muted pink creamy pumps
She wore them on stage
With her jeans
T-shirt and a
Plaid overblouse
She patted her
Patent pumps in time
To the music
She made

Playing her sax
Blowin' her horn for
The Crooked Vines
Just like the boys in the band
She was there to back up
The girl singer
The lead a little too cute
To flaunt sexy
But she got pretty damn close
Tall black boots,
Six inch spikes
Short black dress
Shaking those
Extended Shirley Temple curls
Up town funk you up

Sax comes front and center
Uptown funk you up
Don't believe me just watch
Palm Sunday Eve
Steppin'
One in spiked heels
The other in her Easter shoes
Girls hit you Hallelujah

The Star
by Heather Ann Schmidt

Break me open
Like the inside of a star
Filled with little fires
Of pastel vapor and darkness

The largest black hole is a speck of dirt
In the memory of history

I wish I could borrow the hands of Venus de Milo
But they have been stolen
By war and time

I want this to be the beginning
I look into my breath and walk in that direction
To find what is...

I bend by the waters as an angel woman
And the river leads back to me
And my questions

The prairie is filled with wildflowers
And twilight waiting...

Shame
by Erika Schoeps

You lead me to the sea of red ink—

A day trip with a worn wicker basket
and a half empty bottle of wine.

I feast on the feeling
of your fingers tracing my knuckles;
you go hungry.

Faint stomach half full of ferment,
I slosh towards the shoreline,
stumbling towards thick liquid
too lazy to lap against the sand.

Every unsound step coaxes me further
onto blank paper that curls around
my toes and shaves away skin.

You lean onto abated palms,
watching a precarious sun
tip over and needlessly spill out.

Daylight Returns
by Dennis Shanaberg

The skyline's hid behind curtains of fog.
The sun's stayed dark for far too long,
But frozen lakes boil with coming dawn,
And the pall falls back like shades undrawn.

Light floods planes of lost landscapes
Revealing fields of green and flowered lace.
Color creeps into oppressive grays.
Reborn rivers shout as their cold shells break.

Tomorrow, may the birdcalls take flight,
As the odor of blooms blossom to life,
And the skies finally glow to blue and white
Unto brilliant warm brushstrokes before the coming night.

Error
by Kevin Frederick Smith

Desperate query:
"instant-happiness-dot-com"
"404: Not Found"

Two Places at Once
by Larry Smith

I am driving down old Rte 7
towards Steubenville's
Market Street Bridge.
And as I look out toward
the West Virginia hills,
I am there on that bridge
above the wide Ohio
and I am here in this car
looking out to who I was
and where I've been.
Always a journey this
driving to the "homeplace"
outward and in.

A music in my head
rises from the river,
the hills, the traffic
at this intersection
of presence and memory,
of love and hate at
the beauty and waste.

Standing there once
on the metal grid
tasting the industrial air
looking down at the flowing river
I felt "a river remains,"
wrote it as title for my book.
Now the air is pure yet
the industry abandoned.
The clang and roar
have all gone mute.
Rust and poverty
sting the eyes.
Understanding runs short
as I pass under the bridge
and look up at the cars
rushing over me.

Daylight Savings Time
by Steven B. Smith

The time thieves,
where do they store our stolen hours?

It's blatant theft,
light manipulation,
lugubrious lies from the tardy to slow us early arrivers,
slippery sloppy seconds secluded in dark vaults
accruing nanosecond interest for others,
time not on our side,
used against us,
stolen from sleep under covers of dark,
daylight saving nighttime theft,
add a spring,
subtract a fall,
chronos messing with us all,
the suits saving seconds, minutes, hour,
money time since time is money
and Jesus saves
idle hands from devil torment
sliding round the dial.

At the tone
it will be later than you think,
or too early.

Brief History about Nothing in Particular
by Vladimir Swirynsky

It's illegal to stare at a woman for more than
eight seconds, the penalties unusually harsh.
But wait! I'm only four years old,
it's 1952 and I don't know the difference
between a French kiss and a French horn.
I am modern art, immigration cutie pie,
crying, wanting to be at least thirteen,
to have a quarter in my pocket.
Up in Harlem hip-hop already a century old,
Be Bop nudging Charlie Parker and Billie Holiday
who never found a man without a needle mark.
It was the beats strung out on poetry,
all sorts of crazy shit!
Where the money was, the elite,
this place and that place,
Ivy League and Aztec lords,
they all came to hear the mad sonnets.
This place...
years removed from the songs of Bob Dylan
the psychedelic heartbeat of San Francisco.
This place...
where you couldn't
sit your black ass down
or get a glass of water.

Silent Night, 1914
by Brian Taylor

A sign of truce for the Brits
a beacon — German x-mas trees
both sides laid down their arms
to shake hands with the enemy

A beacon makes all bright
stills the "Great War" to calm
respect sparked that night
and quieted all chance of harm

A silent night until we played
a soccer game with no winner
cheering on the other team
of men we've seen in our mirror

A soccer ball is a handshake
over games with all winners
bouncing ball thru goal posts
of gun-barrels deep in dirt

A dead man's wine for chocolate
gifts of pudding and shoelaces
necklace of empty bullet shells
we showed photos of families

But where's those men who
a gun for x-mas gave to me?
If ever I get them in my sites
I'll thank them appropriately

I'd wish to use my shovel
and make this trench be gone
not my body at the bottom
but a deep grave for my gun

Now if I were to die here
not in any uniform — please
sit me against 2 rifles crossed
a protest for all eternity

I shuda handed over my gun
to my former enemy
I'll stand over and wave good-bye
tho death's not the best of peace

I plan a better peace
than a bullet in the heart
I'll shoot over their heads
assured my brothers do their part

I will miss my friend
in turn he shoots above me
to return each to the love
of our respective families

Next time the bombers fly
instead drop soccer balls
and on the whole world
a better way to fite wars

We will make a square ring
with rifle barrels in the mud
world leaders fite it out
gift popcorn to everyone

Why All Alone?
by Joseph Testa

Why all alone?
Wearing your night down like a smoldering cigarette
when you could be wearing it like a ball gown,
dancing as the ashes fall.
And as the dance floor shrinks and time fleets,
perhaps the night will burn faster.

Now, hand in hand, we dance.
Silhouettes warp the curtains of space.
Passion's weight inhibits the breath,
so we take a harder puff.

And when the head of the night flickers out,
we'll be left with the butt as a reminder.

Heaven
by Steve Thomas

I saw a dog
in ecstasy
the other day

scents from hundreds of miles
away, sucked up his nose
wet tongue hanging
out the window at 45mph

an endless taste of nirvana
interrupted by an occasional sneeze

but not for long, just needed
a moment to adjust those paws
rest that head just so, and away
they went, ears laid back, a sleek

gleam in the eye
lapping up the world.

Drifting Light
by Jonathan Thorn

Last glimpse of heaven
Over the field of grain
The last farewell of the sun
From the last slice of day

Tears of arrows
Part the ground and sky
Seeing what was sown
Drifting into the night

Borrowing Your Shower
by Kerry Trautman

Naked, here, where you are daily naked,
my flesh feels apt to bloom,
fragility watering my leafiness,
my toes rooting to your bathtub bottom.

And if you burst in with hands full of blackberries,
how could I not nuzzle them
from your chalice palms with my wet mouth?

My own water is never this hot, never fizzles
as if giggled from a clown's seltzer bottle.

And if a photographer should splash
the wide wings of me with light,
how could I refuse to still, to pose?

Your mirror flashes me myself in silver dampness,
and there is, somewhere, a piccolo,
armloads of peonies, and nectarines—sliced thinly,
spread across a shortbread tart shell, glistening.

Midnight. West Park Cleveland. April 16.
(Hours Before the Break of Spring)
by Nick Traenkner

In West Park April night
Green buds on tree-tips sleep
Obscured by silhouettes
Who run across the street
Of mischief nighttime spring
To stop on curbs and then
Look back at me.

I crane my neck to stare
Meet eyes through glass and see
Their adolescent beards
Through corner-eye across
My windshield as a song
Of streetlights wide and white
Then red, then green.

The opening air
Holds bare legs blonde
Apartment brick
With hoodied hand
In hoodied hand
Down sidewalk night
Through flowerless air
Before the break
Of leaves.

Then into turns the bumping sways
The wheel each way through curves and holes
The corners, straights and all the way
To the Triskett-Warren Sunoco.

Across the space of empty pumps
In air as much of gas as spring,
A Music floats on perfume tide
Through doors propped wide.
I walk inside

And find a midnight set of men
Silent in flowered air before
The break of spring.

Then back outside in night
Back into empty air
That hums with radios
And flocks of soundless men
And pulling round the pumps
Our couple crosses in
Through air about to bloom
Surrounding everything.

Sonnet 65,000,000 BC
by Mary A. Turzillo

Shall I compare thee to a dinosaur?
Thou art more suave, and less oviparous.
Rough bellows shook cretaceous glens of yore
subduing prey for creatures more carnivorous.

Sometime too hot the breath of raptor steamed,
'fore Ice Age frosted cycad frond and tuft.
Thou'rt still alive, while dino's clock's been cleaned:
by meteor strike the sauropod's been snuffed.

Though featherbrained thou dost sometimes appear,
yet theropods are closer kin to birds
than thee, my own sweet mammal love. So, dear,
I'll praise thee not with roars, but clever words.

    And, long as laser prints and cartridge toner's inked,
    thou shalt not, as the T-Rex, go extinct.

Gasping for Breath
by D.R. Wagner

If the walls hold,
This room will assume
A shape that makes sense.

I could drive a car from
One end of this place to the other.
No traffic lights, just row
After row of houses, lit
In a variety of styles.

I climb into you long,
Your lips, your breasts,
Finally, ourselves again, discovered
Like something lost beneath the sea
Long ago, our pockets full of coins
Engraved with language we
Can no longer read.

I attempt to say something important.
You kiss me on my mouth.
This bliss, a state of grace.
Gasping for breath, I try
To tell you things.
You tell me to shut up.

Far away, tonight, someone
Stands on an overpass above the freeway,
Wanting to die.
Traffic stopped in both directions
On the interstate.

I hold you against me.
We make up songs about
How this feels, so
It becomes easier to understand
What we want to know.

This is one of those songs.
Let's sing it over again
Until it sounds right.

Blue Heron Sonnet
by Mary Weems

For: Gil Scott Heron

He arrived suddenly like jazz, like a
Bopped Bird song, like love—naked as verse.
Raised between the North and South, at war
with himself and every shade of white pow(d)er.
Tracked truth where it lived in disguise.
Music a Valentine, Black bullets, drums.
Government hatred a constant refrain.
His life a short road map, no rainbows.
Revolution elusive as one love,
hip hop, chance of Black life on white moon.
Sixty-two the number for solitude,
bold face aged too soon, mouth, eyes glisten.
He left yesterday on a Black sunrise.
Took twenty-eight minutes to arrive.

After the Fight
by Batya Weinbaum

Thyme
dreams of sadness about you.
John pushes himself against me
I lean back as he points to bicycles on the horizon,
At first, I cannot see them. He thinks me   blind
then they merge into view
bigger than I had expected.
I came down on the side
of ritual and order perhaps against you.
Ellen and I talk of eye exercises,
the politics of food, and at night we read aloud
of poetry, stories and journals.
John reads   Djuna Barnes
Ola cries in the night.
Rosie comes in the morning
the ritual continues
and we move one.

In this dream of sadness, you were wandering.
You came to see me. You were dying, trying
to be tough and strong. We went for ice cream.
I was sorry you were going to be gone
admiring your courage
as I admire Ellen
who pulls herself up on one long rope
dangling over the edge
I am breastfeeding
Ellen is making rituals in the woods
to accept her body scarred, one breast gone.
In the evening in my salon
John is reading aloud
from Djuna Barnes
the night visit to the doctor in drag
who holds forth
about time and the night
and we feel your absence
perplexed about the rashness
of your departure
like a wave in the night.

Earthbound
by Laura Grace Weldon

Are we supposed to settle for a planet
lagging behind our expectations?
We want reversible time,
admission into past or future
easy as changing our minds.
We want teleportation, so we can
zip anywhere for the afternoon,
maybe Iceland or Argentina,
where we'll make new friends,
agree to meet up for lunch
on only an hour's break
next week in Greece.

We want to get past
greed and suffering and war,
enough already.
And death? That's awfully primitive
for souls with so much left to learn.

That said, this planet does a lot right.
Birds, for one.
Water in all its perfect manifestations.
Those alive poems called trees.
The way a moment's glance
can reveal a kindred spirit.

Which we all are, really.
The oneness between self and everything
is this planet's secret, kept imperfectly.
That's more than we might expect.
Although time travel would be nice.

You Undid My Spiral Galaxy & I'm Still Dizzy
by Eva Xanthopoulos

you

                                        into my spiral galaxy

a year or so ago &

                                  the dizzying/hypnotizing

effects still prevail

you

ripped off all my veils
{both material & astral}
without so much as asking   in your emissions
{even when you're physically afar},   i'm still basking

the [he]art of transmutation   **SOLIDIFIED**

in my life fully when you took

my gloomed body & bloomed
it with ela/inspira   -   tion
just by   lockingeyes
with me for a mere moment

you

e
   x

p   l

  o   \ d e a d /

like a super nova without
even moving
your impact on my surface has kept me
ever-grooving

i don't even think you know of the glow
your aura possesses. sweet solar zephyrs
set my tresses swaying

your

inspir   /   exhal   -ations
are much like micro-tantrums
in the sky others mistake
for thunderstorms or
shooting rockets   but i know
what i feel & hear , see & sense
is a love of astronomical proportions
that whirls me , unwinds my spiral galaxy
& opens me up to the Universe   a uni-
verse i was blind   2-fold   to before,
but because of your re-entry into my life,

i now re-remember the ever-expansive

heart/mind/soul of mine that became

further-divine during our celestial
collision on this physical *****✈

Samot
by Shkelaht Yisrael

shy at times
the words are larger than life
simple conversations
on everyday situations
echoing, resonating in my head

no serious questions
or thought-provoking, probing, seeking
wondering imaginations
of what goes on when we are
in the company of others

hellos, goodbyes, how do you dos
"the usual for you
or would you be so bold
as to sample a new item
just this once?"

a smile, eyes touch
"thank you, but no
i will take my favorite for the road
but before i go
i just want you to know
i thought of you today"

Acknowledgments

Zachary Scott Hamilton, "Years in a Seahorse" — *Hound* & *Rasavada*.

Geoffrey A. Landis, "Shout" — *The Squire: Page-A-Day Poetry Anthology 2015* (Writing Knights Press) & the chapbook *The Book of Whimsy* (NightBallet Press, 2015).

Lennart Lundh, "Elegy" — *Deep Water Literary Review*, *The Poetry Storehouse* & the chapbook *So Careless About Themselves* (Writing Knights Press, 2014).

Philip Metres, "Compline" — *Sand Opera* (Alice James Books, 2015) & *Poetry* magazine.

Marisa Moks-Unger, "Lanterns over Lido" — *Mud and Stars* (NightBallet Press, 2015)

rjs, "We Won" — *Collateral Damage: the lost books of rjs* (Iniquity Press, 2007)

D.R. Wagner, "Gasping for Breath" — *The Night Market* (Crisis Chronicles Press, 2014).